D0500740

KRISTALLNACHT, THE NIGHT OF BROKEN GLASS

Igniting the Nazi War Against Jews

by Stephanie Fitzgerald

SNAPSHOTS IN HISTORY

KRISTALLNACHT, THE NIGHT OF BROKEN GLASS

Igniting the Nazi War Against Jews

by Stephanie Fitzgerald

Content Adviser: Steve Remy, Ph.D., Associate
Professor of History, Brooklyn College and Graduate
Center, City University of New York

Reading Adviser: Susan Kesselring, M.A., Literacy Educator,
Rosemount-Apple Valley-Eagan (Minnesota) School District

Compass Point Books ◆ Minneapolis, Minnesota

COMPASS POINT BOOKS

3109 West 50th Street, #115
Minneapolis, MN 55410

 This book was manufactured with paper containing
at least 10 percent post-consumer waste.

For Compass Point Books
Brenda Haugen, XNR Productions, Inc., Catherine Neitge,
Keith Griffin, Lori Bye, and Nick Healy

Produced by White-Thomson Publishing Ltd.

For White-Thomson Publishing
Stephen White-Thomson, Susan Crean, Amy Sparks,
Tinstar Design Ltd., Steve Remy, Peggy Bresnick Kendler,
Brian Fitzgerald, Barbara Bakowski, and Timothy Griffin

Library of Congress Cataloging-in-Publication Data
Fitzgerald, Stephanie.
  Kristallnacht, the night of broken glass: igniting the Nazi War
against Jews / by Stephanie Fitzgerald.
      p. cm.
  Includes bibliographical references and index.
  ISBN 978-0-7565-3489-9 (library binding)
1. Kristallnacht, 1938—Juvenile literature. 2. Jews—Germany—
History—1933–1945—Juvenile literature. 3. Holocaust, Jewish
(1939-1945)—Germany—Juvenile literature. 4. Jews—Persecutions—
Germany—Juvenile literature. I. Title.
  DS134.255.F58 2008
  940.53'1842—dc22   2007032701

Visit Compass Point Books on the Internet at
www.compasspointbooks.com
or e-mail your request to
custserv@compasspointbooks.com

Contents

The Nazi Night of Terror

Chapter

1

On the night of November 9, 1938, in cities and towns throughout Germany and Austria, smoke from burning synagogues filled the sky. Broken furniture, shredded books, and shattered glass littered the streets. Jewish children were awakened from their sleep by the sound of their front doors being broken down and boot steps on the stairs. Jewish men were beaten, arrested, and even killed as their families watched in horror.

Kristallnacht, the night of broken glass, was a pogrom designed by the Nazi leadership to "encourage" Jewish people to leave Germany and Austria. Members of the Nazi government's private army—known as the *Sturmabteilung* (SA), or storm troopers—were given permission to destroy Jewish homes and businesses and anything else owned by Jews.

In the early morning hours of November 10, 1938, Jewish shop owners all over Germany and Austria cleaned up what was left of their businesses.

During the Kristallnacht pogrom, the SA set fire to Jewish community centers and tossed furniture from second-story apartments as local police stood by and watched. Firefighters stood idly by while synagogues burned. They only turned on their hoses to keep the fires from spreading to non-Jewish property. Ordinary German citizens stopped to throw rocks through store windows while others hurried past with their faces turned away from the destruction. A few brave souls hid their Jewish neighbors in their homes.

Rudy Bamber was a young Jewish boy living in the city of Nuremberg, Germany, in 1938. He later remembered what happened to his family on the morning of November 10:

> In the early hours of the morning [they] broke the front door down and started to smash the place up. ... We had two lots [of storm troopers]. One lot just concentrated on smashing things up and left. And then the second lot arrived. Three elderly ladies were living on the first floor with us. One was dragged out and beaten

POGROMS

A pogrom is an organized attack against a minority group, particularly Jewish people. It comes from the Russian word *pogromit*, which means "to wreak havoc." Although pogroms took place as far back as the Middle Ages, the word came out of a series of attacks against Jews that took place in Russia in the late 19th and early 20th centuries. One such pogrom took place in the city of Chisinau in 1903 and resulted in the deaths of 45 Jews. Pogroms in Russia increased in violence and frequency starting in 1905. By 1917, the practice had ended there. Pogroms were later revived by German Nazis.

for no reason. .... And I was sort of knocked about and finally ended up in the cellar. ... When I came out I went back upstairs and found my father dying. Dead. I tried as far as I could artificial respiration, but ... it was too late. I was absolutely in shock. ... They didn't know me. They had no grudge against me. They were just people who had come to do whatever they thought they should do.

The Berlin fire department tried to keep the flames of a synagogue (left) from spreading to a nearby home but did nothing to protect the Jewish house of worship.

11

Hugh Carleton Green, a correspondent who worked for London's *Daily Telegraph* and was based in the city of Berlin, described what he saw during Kristallnacht:

Jewish-owned businesses in Berlin lay in shambles after the pogrom.

> *Mob law ruled in Berlin throughout the afternoon and evening and hordes of hooligans*

> *indulged in an orgy of destruction. I have seen several anti-Jewish outbreaks in Germany during the last five years, but never anything as nauseating as this. Racial hatred and hysteria seemed to have taken complete hold of otherwise decent people. I saw fashionably dressed women clapping their hands and screaming with glee, while respectable, middle-class mothers held up their babies to see the "fun."*

Nazi leadership tried to pretend that Kristallnacht had been initiated and carried out by German and Austrian citizens. Although some ordinary citizens did seize the chance to wreak havoc on their Jewish neighbors, the idea for the pogrom had come directly from the top. Adolf Hitler had given verbal orders to Joseph Goebbels, who was the head of Nazi propaganda. Goebbels then personally passed along the orders for the attacks.

The November pogrom came to be known as the night of broken glass because the streets were littered with shattered windows from the Jewish homes, businesses, and synagogues that had been destroyed. At the time, Germany did not produce its own plate glass for windows. It imported the glass from other countries. It took a Belgian company six months to replace all the glass that had been broken.

During Kristallnacht, close to 8,000 Jewish-owned stores, warehouses, and homes were destroyed. Hundreds of synagogues were demolished, the

The Fasanenstrasse Synagogue in Berlin was one of many synagogues destroyed by fire on November 9, 1938.

majority by fire, and more than 100 Jews were killed. An additional 30,000 were sent to concentration camps.

Jews had been persecuted in Germany for years—financially, socially, and even physically. But Kristallnacht marked a turning point. The pogrom was carried out on a massive scale—and on the world stage. It was reported in newspapers all over Europe and the United States. No one—either in Germany or elsewhere in the world—took steps to intervene on behalf of the Jewish people living in Austria and Germany.

Kristallnacht sent a clear message to the world that the Nazis wanted the Jews out of Germany and its territories and that they would go to bloody lengths to achieve that goal. There was also a message for the people who supported the Nazis: No matter how hard they pushed the Jews, no one in the world would try to stop them. ◣

A Breeding Ground for Hatred

Chapter 2

In the years immediately after World War I (1914–1918), Germany was on the brink of ruin. The Great War, as it was called at the time, had taken a terrible toll on many European nations, especially France. More than 8 million people died as a result of the war, and much of the French countryside was destroyed. When Germany finally surrendered, its enemies made Germany pay dearly for the war it had played a large part in starting. They wanted to make sure that Germany would never be strong enough to start another war.

After World War I ended, many Germans blamed not just the victorious Allies for their plight. Encouraged by politicians such as Hitler, many Germans blamed their Jewish countrymen as well.

After World War I, Germany's air fleet was dismantled, and the wooden airplane propellers were cut up and used for firewood.

THE GREAT WAR

The spark that started World War I was the assassination of Franz Ferdinand, archduke of Austria-Hungary, by a Bosnian–Serb nationalist. After that incident, both countries called on their allies. Germany supported Austria. Russia, France, and Great Britain sided with the Serbs. The first shots of World War I were fired on August 2, 1914, by German soldiers who invaded Belgium on their way to attack France. In this conflict, Russia, France, and Great Britain were referred to as the Allies.

Many Germans thought that Jews were responsible for what they felt was a premature end to the war. They believed that their soldiers had not lost the war on the battlefield. They claimed that the Jews had betrayed German soldiers by pushing the government to surrender and sign the Treaty of Versailles, the peace treaty that ended the war.

Of course, that claim was false. The leadership of the German army demanded that the government seek terms of surrender because that army was no longer able to continue fighting. German military leaders and certain politicians deliberately hid this information, though. They claimed that German Jews and members of different political parties had pressured the government to surrender.

Germans referred to this "forced" surrender as the *Dolchstoss*, meaning "stab in the back." Because the war ended in November 1918, they referred to Jews, liberals, and socialists as the November criminals. Many people in Germany—and all over Europe— were anti-Semitic. They hated Jewish people and wanted to blame the Jews for all of their problems. A belief in the Dolchstoss led to an increase in anti-Semitism in Germany.

At the end of World War I, the Treaty of Versailles required Germany to give up all its colonies and hand over large portions of land, mainly to France and the new state of Poland. Portions of Germany

The Treaty of Versailles was signed in the Hall of Mirrors in the Palace of Versailles, in France, as Allied officers looked on from outside.

19

were to be occupied by Allied forces and were required to remain demilitarized, or allowed to keep only a limited army. Germany, which from 1918 until 1933 became known as the Weimer Republic, was also forced to pay reparations of 132 billion gold reichsmarks—more than $35 billion.

Many Germans felt that the Treaty of Versailles was unfair. They believed that Germany had never been defeated on the battlefield and therefore should not have surrendered. This belief led to the rise of new political parties. Among them was the National Socialist German Worker's Party, or Nazi Party. It was led by Adolf Hitler, a former World War I German army corporal who attempted a coup d'état, or government overthrow, in Munich in November 1923.

On November 8, 1923, a group of armed Nazi Party members led by Hitler interrupted a political meeting conducted by Gustav von Kahr, the dictator of Bavaria. This large southern German state was home to the Nazi Party and many other political groups. Though no shots were fired at the time, Hitler called for a new national government, which he would lead.

The coup, which became known as the Beer Hall Putsch, was unsuccessful. The Nazis left the meeting without having accomplished anything. At 11 the next morning, Hitler led his followers in a march on Munich. Since many of the Nazi Party's members had served in World War I, Hitler thought they would have the support of the police. He was wrong. The Nazis were stopped at the city center by the police. During the standoff, someone fired a shot, which killed a police sergeant. The police responded by opening fire on the demonstrators. In less than one minute, the Nazis' coup was over. Three policemen and 16 Nazis were killed, and many others were wounded.

A crowd gathered to hear a speaker at the Beer Hall Putsch in Munich.

21

Hitler was one of the first people to flee the scene. He hid in a friend's home for two days before he was found and arrested. For his part in the coup, Hitler was sentenced to five years in prison—the minimum possible sentence. While he was in prison, Hitler wrote a book called *Mein Kampf*, meaning "My Struggle," which outlined his plans for Germany and his anti-Semitic attitude toward Jews. On December 20, 1924, after less than nine months in jail, Hitler was released on parole.

Two months later, Hitler was back at the helm of the Nazi Party. This time, thanks to the failure of the Beer Hall Putsch, Hitler was determined to gain power legally, through the ballot box. He made no secret of his intentions to replace the democratic government with a new regime.

The political unrest in Germany was partly caused by the country's failing economy. Though the economy stabilized briefly in the mid-1920s, a

A WORLD IN CRISIS

The Great Depression of the 1930s was unique—it was an economic downturn that affected the whole world rather than just one nation. Individual countries tried to boost their own industries by attaching high tariffs, or import taxes, on foreign goods. This plan was flawed, though, because it effectively stopped foreign trade, which made the depression drag on for years. According to estimates, 30 million people around the world were unemployed by 1932. In countries such as Germany, Italy, and Japan, this instability led to the rise of fascism—a form of dictatorship.

German workers baled money as if it were hay. German currency was worth more as waste paper than as money.

global depression soon brought crippling economic hardship to the entire world. Desperate times once again brought social unrest to Germany and opened the doors to extreme political parties.

As life in Germany became more desperate, Hitler's popularity grew. Like others in the country, he blamed Germany's problems on the Treaty of Versailles and, in effect, on the Jews. Hitler gained followers and strength with his promises

23

to not only restore Germany's position in the world but also to raise the country to new heights of power. Hitler's entire philosophy revolved around his bitter anti-Semitism, which he made a central point of the Nazi Party's system of beliefs.

The Nazi Party platform was built upon total devotion to the German nation and anti-Semitism. Hitler intended to get back all Germany had lost through the Treaty of Versailles. He promised to revive the economy and restore Germany's greatness by rebuilding the armed forces and expanding the country's borders. A key to this plan was to populate Germany with only "pure" Aryans.

WIDESPREAD HATRED

Anti-Semitism is one of the defining characteristics of Nazism in general and Adolf Hitler in particular. But Hitler did not invent prejudice or discrimination against Jews. By the end of the 19th century, anti-Semitism was widespread throughout Europe, not just in Germany. It was rooted in the belief that Jewish people were of a different—and inferior—race. Many people wrongly believed that Jews were biologically different from non-Jews.

Hitler believed that German-speaking European people belonged to an Aryan race, which was superior to all other ethnic groups. He believed that Jews were the most inferior race of all. Hitler's desire to create a "pure" Germany made up of only Aryans hinged on the idea of ridding the country of non-Aryans, especially Jews. The non-Aryan designation included all minorities, as well as mentally ill and physically handicapped people. Hitler also believed that Aryans were responsible

for all the advances in world history and that Jews wanted to destroy everything the Aryans had built—or take it over. This was another idea of anti-Semitism: the belief that Jews held too much power and were responsible for everything bad that happened in the world.

Adolf Hitler's popularity grew steadily throughout Germany in the 1920s and early 1930s.

25

Jewish people in Germany worked in and ran businesses, such as this wholesale fruit business in Berlin.

The official name for Nazi Germany was the Third Reich, or empire. Hitler referred to the Nazi reign as the Thousand-Year Reich because he believed the party's power would last for 1,000 years. As far as Hitler was concerned, the only thing standing in the way of the Thousand-Year Reich was the Jews.

Anti-Semitism was common in Germany, as it was in much of the world, but many Jews living in Germany had worked hard to become a part of German society. In 1933, about 500,000 Jews were living in Germany. About one-fifth of them were not German citizens. They were immigrants from Eastern Europe, mainly Poland. Whether they were citizens or not, most of these people were deeply patriotic and a part of mainstream German society. Many German Jews were poor, but there was a strong Jewish middle class. Most Jewish people owned or worked in small businesses, especially stores such as clothing or furniture shops, or were doctors and lawyers.

Though Hitler's ideas must have made them uncomfortable, no one in the Jewish community could have guessed the depth of his hatred for Jews or the lengths to which he would go to force them out of Germany.

By the mid-1930s, Hitler's plans would start to become clearer. German Jews had much to fear from the man who was on the way to becoming absolute dictator of Germany's Third Reich. ◣

The Rise of the Nazis

Chapter

3

The Nazis had tried, on several occasions, to win election to government positions. But they did not have much success until 1930, when they received 18 percent of the total vote. Thanks to that victory, the Nazis went from the smallest party in Germany to the second largest.

In 1932, Hitler ran for president of Germany but ultimately lost to Paul von Hindenburg. In January 1933, President Hindenburg appointed Hitler chancellor. Although the chancellor was the head of the democratic government, Hindenburg hoped that giving Hitler the position would keep the Nazis under control. In his position as chancellor, Hitler would have to work with the other political parties in the government. But, Hindenburg's plan would eventually backfire.

Hoping to control the Nazi Party, President Paul von Hindenburg (right) appointed Hitler chancellor of Germany.

Hitler became dictator of Germany in March and quickly began wielding his power against the Jews. On April 1, 1933, the Nazi Party organized a nationwide boycott of Jewish businesses. Lists of Jewish stores and shops were printed and handed out in every town so people would know which to avoid. The Star of David was painted on the fronts of Jewish-owned shops, as were swastikas—the symbol of the Nazi Party—and the word *Jude*, the German word for "Jew." Messages such as "Jews Out!" and "Perish Jews" were written across the fronts of Jewish-owned stores. People were encouraged to report on Germans who ignored the boycott, and SA troops stood outside Jewish businesses to threaten anyone who tried to enter.

Despite these efforts, the average German citizen did not support the boycott. Many even actively defied it by going out of their way to visit Jewish-owned businesses. The failed boycott was quickly canceled after the first day.

Less than a week later, on April 7, Hitler introduced the Law for the Restoration of a Professional Civil Service. Under this law, only Aryans could hold civil service, or government, jobs. All non-Aryans were either fired or forced to retire.

On April 21, the Jewish way of preparing meat—called kosher butchering—was outlawed. This made life difficult for Orthodox Jews, who

Nazi Party members encouraged anti-Semitic graffiti on Jewish businesses.

ate only meats that were prepared according to Jewish law. Despite the threat of severe punishment, many Jews resisted this law.

Schlomo Wahrmann's father, who was trained as a kosher butcher, slaughtered meat for the people in his community in the city of Leipzig at great risk to himself and his family. Wahrmann, who was a child at the time, later wrote about this experience:

> *Often, my younger sister would carry the [koshering knife] to the chicken market because we were confident the Gestapo [secret police] would not apprehend such a young girl. Nonetheless, my mother remained tense.*

31

Orthodox Jews who could not obtain kosher meat had to learn to live without it. Jewish newspapers in Germany printed vegetarian recipes, and two years later, in 1935, Germany's League of Jewish Women published a cookbook with vegetarian meals.

Though groups and individuals tried to resist Nazi rule, it was difficult at best. The Gestapo terrorized Jews—and there was no one to stop the abuse. People were beaten and arrested on phony charges on a whim. But it was not just the Nazi government or its police who were threats. Nazi propaganda had convinced many Germans that Jews were the enemy. Jewish people had to live in constant fear that even if they escaped the notice of the Gestapo, they could be reported by their neighbors and arrested for any made-up charge.

On April 25, 1933, a law was passed prohibiting the overcrowding of German schools, which limited the number of Jewish students who could enroll in public schools. More discriminatory laws followed, all with the same intention. Hitler was determined to isolate and

THE PROPAGANDA PARTY

Propaganda is information, often false, that is spread to make people believe in a certain cause. The Nazis used propaganda extensively to gain the support of German citizens. Joseph Goebbels was head of the Nazi Propaganda Ministry. The ministry controlled all forms of communication in Germany, including newspapers, books, magazines, music, movies, radio, and public meetings. A big part of Goebbels' job was to spread and inflame feelings of anti-Semitism among the German people.

harass the half million Jews living in Germany to the point where they would want to leave the country. At this time in history, the Nazis were not focused on the mass murder of Jews—they wanted to make Germany *Judenfrei*, meaning "Jew free," or *Judenrein*, meaning "pure of Jews."

On May 10, books by Jewish authors and others the Nazis did not approve of were burned in huge bonfires in front of several German universities. Jewish artists were no longer allowed to exhibit their work in public galleries. Like Hitler's political enemies, thousands of Jews were arrested and thrown into concentration camps. These were prison camps where inmates were forced to work and live under terrible conditions. Vicious beatings and murder became increasingly common. By the end of 1933, more than 30 Jews had been killed.

After President Hindenburg died in August 1934, Hitler combined the positions of president and chancellor and named himself *führer*, or absolute ruler of Germany. The democratic constitution was disposed of and replaced by a one-party dictatorship. Hitler immediately cracked down on his political enemies, who—by his orders—were arrested, shot, or bludgeoned to death by the SA. In 1934, Hitler even purged his own party of those he feared might challenge his authority. In a single night in June 1934, Hitler cleaned out the SA leadership. This purge became known as the Night of the Long Knives.

The Nazis and their supporters burned thousands of books written by non-Aryans.

Hitler quickly started on his quest to make Germany the most powerful nation in the world. Completely disregarding the provisions of the Treaty of Versailles, Hitler created a new army, navy, and air force. Hitler's focus, however, remained on creating a superior nation made up of only "pure" Germans. The Nazi policy was to encourage all non-Aryans, specifically Jews, to leave Germany.

In addition to being forced to live under racist laws, Jews were often subjected to harsh discrimination from other Germans. Many

FORCED TO FLEE

As pressure on Jews increased, some of Germany's greatest thinkers were forced into exile.

- Bertolt Brecht, who was best known for writing *The Threepenny Opera*, was one of Germany's most important writers. After his books and plays were banned in Germany, he fled to Denmark.

- Thomas Mann, who wrote *The Magic Mountain* and *Death in Venice*, won the Nobel Prize in literature in 1929. Though not Jewish himself, he was married to a Jew. Mann was out of the country when the Nazis rose to power, and he chose not to return. Though he was no fan of the Nazis, Mann's desire to keep his books from being banned in Germany prevented him from speaking out against the government.

- In 1933, after the Nazis seized his property, Albert Einstein, winner of the Nobel Prize in physics, fled to Belgium. He immigrated to the United States in October of that year.

Germans claimed they could tell who was a Jew just by looking at a person—or because they believed that Jewish people smelled like garlic.

Strangers felt no shame in publicly pointing out people they thought were Jewish by commenting on their looks or smell. Some Jewish people found small satisfaction in showing the stupidity of people like this. Historian Marion Kaplan wrote about one such incident:

> *In one case, a woman remarked upon three children seated across from her in a train compartment. She admired the two "Aryan" types and denigrated [belittled] the darker girl. The father of the two finally told her that the two blonds had a Jewish mother and the darker one was "Aryan."*

35

Throughout 1934 and 1935, the Nazis continued to apply pressure to Germany's Jewish citizens. Signs reading "Jews Not Wanted" started to appear in hotels, theaters, sports stadiums, and restaurants. Similar signs were posted on the roads leading into various villages.

The Nazis hung banners telling Aryan citizens, "Germans, do not buy from Jews."

On September 15, 1935, racial discrimination and hatred were formalized in the Nuremberg Laws. These laws decreed that Jews were not German citizens and prohibited them from marrying or having sexual relationships with anyone of German blood. Jews were also forbidden to fly the German flag.

By making life as difficult as possible for the Jews, the Nazis hoped that Jewish people would be forced to emigrate, eventually making Germany "Judenfrei." Nazi policy was successful to a certain degree—Jewish people were leaving Germany at a rate of about 25,000 per year from 1934 to 1937. By 1938, more than one-quarter of Germany's Jewish population had left the country. ◣

CREATING CULTURE

When Jews were excluded from the cultural life of Germany, they created their own. Individual synagogues hosted lectures, plays, and symphonies performed by Jewish artists. The Jewish Cultural Association, which was founded in 1933, provided entertainment to its nearly 70,000 members and also created employment for Jewish artists who had lost their jobs.

Building Toward Disaster

Chapter

4

At the same time his plan for pushing the Jews out of Germany was unfolding, Hitler was pursuing the other part of his dream—building an empire. On March 7, 1936, Hitler's troops marched into the Rhineland, an area to the west of Germany near the borders of Belgium, Luxembourg, and France. According to the Treaty of Versailles, this area was to be demilitarized. No German military forces were permitted to be stationed in the Rhineland. Despite this, no armies opposed the Nazi troops.

Other Western European countries were still shell-shocked from World War I. The long, bloody conflict had cost them much—both financially and in lives lost. Rather than confront Hitler, British Prime Minister Neville Chamberlain and French Foreign Minister Georges Bonnet

On March 7, 1936, Germany re-occupied the Rhineland—against the provisions of the Treaty of Versailles—as Nazi troops marched into Düsseldorf, Germany.

attempted to appease him. They thought that if they gave Hitler what he wanted, he would stop demanding more. But the opposite was true. The more he got away with, the more invincible Hitler felt. This would have dire consequences for the world at large and for German Jews in particular.

During this time, Jewish persecution had slowed down a bit. Germany was hosting the 1936 Summer Olympics, and Hitler did not want the world to see the harsh reality—the concentration camps, the anti-Jewish graffiti, the boycotts, and the abuse—that existed there for Jews. Things remained relatively quiet in 1937, leading some people to believe that the situation in Germany was getting better. But this was just the calm before the storm.

With the Western powers reluctant to oppose him, Hitler was growing confident. He was ready to pursue his dream of a German empire. First he had to get the members of the Nazi Party fired up. The best way to do this was to once again increase pressure on the Jews. That was not the only reason Hitler needed to re-establish his campaign of terror, though.

JESSE OWENS

Hitler saw the 1936 Olympics as an opportunity to show the world the superiority of the Aryan race. That plan was destroyed, however, by American track-and-field star Jesse Owens. Hitler had no respect for Owens, who was an African-American, an ethnic group that the führer considered "non-human." Owens struck a blow against racism when he won four gold medals at the games—beating athletes from Hitler's supposed superior race.

In February 1938, at a meeting with Austrian Chancellor Kurt von Schuschnigg, Hitler demanded more power for the Nazi Party in Austria. Schuschnigg refused and was eventually forced to resign his post by members of the party.

The cover of a German brochure from the 1936 Berlin Olympics featured an illustration of the Nazis' Aryan ideal.

Arthur Seyss-Inquart, the leader of the Austrian Nazi Party, took over and, on March 13, invited the German army to occupy Austria. The result was a union between Germany and Austria, called *Anschluss*. When Austria's population was incorporated into the Third Reich, the number of Jews increased by almost 200,000. This was nearly equal to the total number of Jews who had been forced to emigrate from Germany in the early 1930s.

Most non-Jewish citizens of Austria at that time were highly anti-Semitic, but anti-Jewish activity had been kept in check by the government. Once Seyss-Inquart took over, though, the situation changed drastically.

On March 11, 1938, knowing the Germans would soon occupy their country, Austrian Nazis took to the streets of Vienna in a violent frenzy that would last for days. The police did nothing to stop them. In many cases, they merely stood by and watched.

Any Jewish person caught on the streets was beaten or humiliated. Some were forced to clean out army toilets while wearing their sacred prayer bands, special strips of cloth they wore on their arms. Jewish businesses were destroyed—their windows smashed and the goods inside stolen.

A shocking number of Jewish people committed suicide. A report in *The New York Times* stated that up to 170 Jews were taking their own lives every

Austrian women waved swastikas to show their support for the union of Austria and Germany following the German occupation.

day. Thousands more ran from the violence, immigrating to neighboring countries or even as far away as Great Britain and the United States when they could.

Nazi Party members in Germany were impressed by the work of their comrades in Vienna in shrinking

43

The graffiti on Jewish shops in Austria warned the owners that if they cleaned up the hateful slogans, they would be sent to a concentration camp.

the Jewish population. The *Schwarze Korps*, a weekly Nazi newspaper, reported:

> *They have managed to do overnight what we have failed to do up to this day in the slow-moving, ponderous north. In Austria, a boycott of the Jews does not need organizing—the people themselves have instituted it with honest joy.*

CAUGHT IN THE MIDDLE

In September 1938, Czechoslovakia became a victim of Europe's hopes to keep Hitler happy. Hitler was insisting that the Sudetenland should be under German control. The region had been a part of Germany until after World War I, when it became part of Czechoslovakia. When the heads of state of Germany, Great Britain, France, and Italy met in Munich to discuss the situation, the head of Czechoslovakia was not invited. At the meeting, the leaders signed an agreement that transferred the Sudetenland to Germany. When Czechoslovakia's president, Eduard Benes, protested the decision, he was told by Great Britain's leadership that they were not willing to go to war with Germany over the Sudetenland.

In the months that followed, Austrians would devote this "joy" to raising the humiliation and persecution of Jews to nearly unimaginable levels.

On March 23, after 11 days of Nazi rule in Austria, U.S. President Franklin Delano Roosevelt invited representatives from around the world to set up a special committee to help political refugees emigrate from Austria and Germany. Of all the countries gathered at the conference in Evian, France, only the Dominican Republic offered to increase the quota of immigrants it would allow inside its borders.

The other countries did not just refuse to raise the number of refugees to whom they would offer shelter; in reality, they lowered the number of immigrants they would allow. Countries such as the United States made it their policy for immigration to be as difficult as possible for Jewish refugees.

Officials would demand documents they knew would be impossible for the immigrants to get or would simply reject applications outright.

President Roosevelt had good intentions for calling the conference and trying to solve the problem of Jewish refugees. But his power was not absolute. He had to answer to the people who had elected him. Like many people around the world, numerous members of the U.S. government were anti-Semitic. They were also in the middle of a depression. As a result, they feared that allowing millions of unemployed immigrants into the country would cause competition for the few jobs available to U.S. citizens. For the same reasons, a large portion of the American public opposed letting Jews into the country. The Evian Conference was a failure.

A PLACE TO CALL HOME

As part of the peace agreement made after World War I, Palestine, an area of the Middle East, was handed over to Great Britain to govern. In the 1920s and beyond, many Jews had immigrated to the area to create a Jewish state. In the late 1930s, German Jews saw Palestine as the perfect place to which they could escape. Many knew they would feel like outsiders at worst, or visitors at best, in other countries. However, in moving to Palestine, they would feel as if they were going to a place where they would truly be welcomed. But it was the British government, not the Jews living there, that decided who would be allowed into Palestine.

Between 1933 and 1939, approximately 85,000 German and Austrian Jews were taken in by the United States, and more than 50,000 settled in Palestine. Though Palestine was preferable to

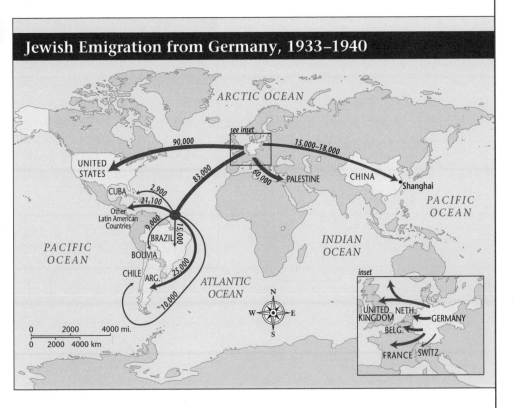

Jewish Emigration from Germany, 1933–1940

many Jews, the British government set severe restrictions on the number of immigrants who would be accepted.

As fewer European nations agreed to accept refugees, tens of thousands of German, Austrian, and Polish Jews made their way to Shanghai, China, one of the few places that did not have visa requirements.

The Evian Conference had accomplished little, but the effect it had on Hitler was chilling. Once again he was convinced that he had nothing to fear from the other nations of the world. And he realized that the leaders of these nations would do little or nothing in defense of Germany's Jews.

German and Austrian Jews sought refuge all over the world, ultimately producing the widest diaspora, or dispersion, of any people in history.

Nazi leaders were frustrated by their inability to force all of the Jews from Germany. One of the reasons the Nazis had increased the persecution of Jews in 1938 was to force them to emigrate. But now, in effect, the rest of the world was telling the Jews they had to stay in Germany.

THE *ST. LOUIS*

In 1939, about 900 Jewish refugees sailed from Hamburg, Germany, aboard the *St. Louis*. After being turned away by Cuba and the United States, the ship was forced to return to Europe, where its passengers disembarked in Belgium. In the end, most of the passengers died in concentration camps or death camps.

There was nowhere else for them to go. No country was willing to take them. Nazi leaders realized they had to take more drastic action to rid their country of the Jewish population they so despised.

On April 26, 1938, Hermann Goering, economic dictator of Germany, declared that all Jewish holdings valued at more than 5,000 reichsmarks (approximately $1,200) would have to be registered. In this way, he would have a record of all the Jewish wealth in Germany. Sixth months later he declared that all Jewish businesses had to be marked as being Jewish owned.

In 1939, Gilbert J. Kraus, an attorney from Philadelphia, paid for 50 German children to come to the United States. Almost 60 families in the area offered to adopt or care for the refugees.

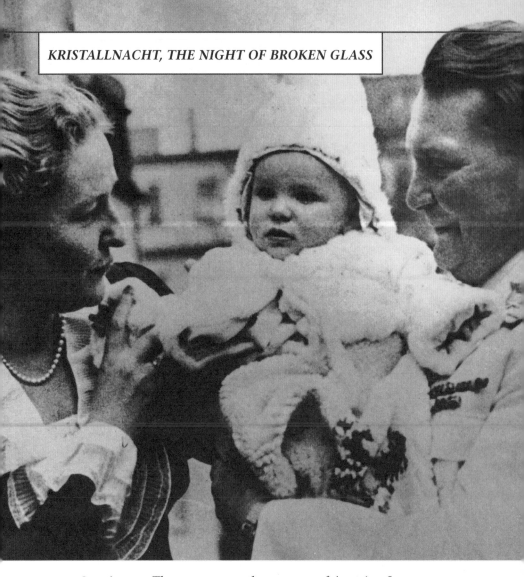

Soon after declaring that all Jewish businesses had to be marked, Hermann Goering celebrated his 46th birthday with his wife Emmy and their daughter Edda.

That same month, a group of Austrian Jews were dragged into the Prater, an amusement park in Vienna, Austria, and forced to eat grass, chirp like birds, and run in circles until they collapsed on the ground. Others were buckled into the roller coaster and forced to ride over and over at full speed until they passed out. Some people suffered heart attacks, and others died. Similar "pleasure hours," as the Nazis referred to them, also took place in Frankfurt, Germany.

On June 9, 1938, the main synagogue in Munich, Germany, was burned down. The following day, Joseph Goebbels, the head of Nazi propaganda and cultural dictator, made a secret speech to Berlin's police. "In the coming half year," he said, "the Jews must be forced to leave Berlin. The police are to work hand-in-hand with the party in this."

THE FOUR YEAR PLAN

Hermann Goering was commissioner of the Nazi's Four Year Plan, an economic reform program that placed an emphasis on rebuilding Germany's military. The plan also included public works projects, increased automobile production and synthetic fiber production, and a number of architectural projects, including further development of the autobahn—Germany's national highway system.

Soon after, more than 2,000 Jews throughout the country were arrested on charges of "race pollution." Simply living among the Aryan population was considered a crime. The people who were arrested were brought to one of three concentration camps: Dachau, Buchenwald, or Sachsenhausen.

In the camps, the inmates worked for 14 to 16 hours a day breaking and hauling stones. At Buchenwald and Sachsenhausen, the prisoners worked to enlarge the camps. At Dachau, they were made to sew the Star of David on thousands of striped uniforms.

On August 10, 1938, another synagogue was burned down, this one in Nuremberg. Seven days later, a new law declared that all Jews had to use the name Israel (for a man) or Sarah (for a woman) before their own first names. On September 27,

Prisoners in the concentration camps were given identification numbers and wore striped uniforms with the Star of David sewn onto them.

it became illegal for Jewish attorneys to practice law in Germany. On October 7, German passports belonging to Jews were made invalid. The passports were taken away and replaced by special identity cards.

The Nazis were building toward something even more terrible, slowly pushing the Jews closer to a horrible fate. At a meeting on October 14, 1938,

Goering gave the signal that new, drastic measures were about to begin. "The Reich must eradicate doubtful elements from the population," he told his colleagues. "Namely, the last remaining Jews."

The Nazis would soon deliver a crushing blow to the Jewish people of Germany and Austria. They simply needed to find the right opportunity. Less than a month later, that opportunity was handed to them by a 17-year-old German Jew living in Paris. His name was Herschel Grynszpan. ◣

"I've Just Shot a Man in His Office"

Chapter

5

Herschel Grynszpan was a German-born Jew with Polish parents who was living in Paris with his aunt and uncle in 1938. Almost every day he read stories in the *Pariser Haint*, the Yiddish paper in Paris, about the hardships facing the Jews in Germany.

Because Herschel's family still lived in Germany, he was alarmed to read a report on October 31, 1938, that 12,000 Polish Jews had been deported from Germany. On November 3, he received a postcard from his sister Berta. As Herschel read the postcard, his worst fears were realized. The postcard said:

> *You have undoubtedly heard of our great misfortune. I will give you a description of what happened. On Thursday night there*

were rumors circulating that all Polish Jews of a certain city had been expelled. However, we refused to believe them. On Thursday night at 9 P.M., a Schupo [local policeman] came to our house and told us we had to go to the police headquarters with our passports. We went just as we were, all together, to the police headquarters, accompanied by the Schupo. There we found almost our entire neighborhood already assembled. A police wagon then took us at once to the Rathaus [town hall]. Everyone was taken there. We had not yet been told what it was about, but we quickly realized that it was the end for us. An expulsion order was thrust into our hands. We had to leave Germany before October 29 (Saturday).

Polish Jews who were expelled from Germany had nowhere to live and belonged to no country.

> *We were not allowed to return to our homes.*
> *I begged to be allowed to return home to get*
> *at least a few essential things. So I left with*
> *a Schupo accompanying me and I packed a*
> *valise with the most necessary clothes. That is*
> *all I could save. We don't have a cent.*

The next day Herschel read a newspaper report that filled out Berta's story. The report from Zbonszyn, a small Polish border town, read in part:

> *Critical situation of Polish Jews deported*
> *from Germany. More than 8,000 persons*
> *have overnight been made stateless. They*
> *were rounded up and deported, largely to*
> *Zbonszyn, in no-man's-land between Germany*
> *and Poland. Their living conditions are*
> *uncomfortable and distressing. 1,200 of them*
> *have fallen ill and several hundred are without*
> *shelter. … A number of cases of insanity and*
> *suicide have been reported.*

Herschel was filled with anger and despair. It made him sick to think of his family being treated so badly. At 8:35 A.M. on Monday, November 7, Herschel decided to take matters into his own hands. He arrived at A La Fine Lame ("At the Sharp Blade"), a store that sold guns and ammunition, just as it was opening.

After buying a gun from the owner, who told the young man how to load and fire the weapon, Herschel set out again. He was supposed to fill out a declaration form for his gun and hand it in to the police. Herschel never made it to the police station, though. Instead he went to a café that he often visited with friends. He unwrapped his gun and loaded five cartridges in the chambers.

By 9:30 A.M., Herschel had reached his destination—the German Embassy. He asked to see the German ambassador and was told he was not in. At that same moment, a man walked past Herschel on his way out of the embassy. It was the ambassador, Count Johannes von Welczeck. He had heard Herschel ask for him but did not want to interrupt his morning walk, so he didn't stop. That decision likely saved his life.

Once inside the embassy, Herschel told porter Henri Nagorka that he had an important document and needed to see someone who knew German secrets. Nagorka took Herschel to see Ernst vom Rath, the only official who was on duty that early in the morning.

When vom Rath asked to see Herschel's document, the young man reached into the inside pocket of his jacket and pulled out his gun. "You

> ### A DESPERATE MESSAGE
>
> On Monday morning, before he left for the gun shop, Herschel Grynszpan wrote a note to his aunt and uncle on the back of a photograph of himself that he kept in his wallet. He started the note in Hebrew with the words "with God's help." Then he continued in German: "My dear relatives, I couldn't do otherwise. God must forgive me. My heart bleeds when I think of our tragedy and that of the 12,000 Jews. I have to protest in such a way that the whole world hears my protest, and this I intend to do. I beg your forgiveness."

are a *sale boche* [filthy kraut, an offensive word for a German] and here, in the name of 12,000 persecuted Jews, is your document!" he screamed.

Herschel fired five shots at vom Rath at point-blank range, hitting him twice. To Herschel's surprise, the diplomat did not die. Vom Rath staggered to his feet calling for help. Herschel just stood there staring at his victim. He made no attempt to attack vom Rath again.

Herschel Grynszpan was arrested within moments after shooting Ernst vom Rath.

Upon hearing the shots and vom Rath's calls for help, Nagorka came running. More help arrived as a doctor and a French policeman named Auret were called to the scene. Through all the excitement, Herschel just sat quietly in a chair.

On the way to the police station, Herschel spoke to Officer Auret. "I've just shot a man in his office," he said. "I do not regret it. I did it to avenge my parents, who are living in misery in Germany."

Herschel's act of vengeance would do more harm than good for his family—and all of the Jews living in Germany. The attack would provide the Nazis with an excuse to wreak havoc throughout Germany, causing the suffering of thousands of families just like Herschel's.

As soon as news of the shooting reached Hitler, he ordered his personal physician to Paris to take care of vom Rath. Despite the doctor's best attempts, vom Rath died on November 9, 1938, at 4:25 P.M. ◣

Lighting the Fuse

Chapter 6

The Nazis would blame Herschel Grynszpan in particular and Jews in general for Kristallnacht. They would claim that Germans were outraged about the assassination of vom Rath and took it out on the country's Jews. This was typical Nazi propaganda. In reality, the pogrom carried out on the evening of November 9 and the following day was ordered by the men at the highest levels in the Nazi Party, including Adolf Hitler and Joseph Goebbels.

The timing of Grynszpan's attack on vom Rath could not have been worse. November 9, the day vom Rath died, was one of the most important dates in Nazi Party history—and in 1938 it was especially significant. November 9, 1938, was the 20th anniversary of the Dolchstoss—the alleged "stab in the back" that led to Germany's surrender in World War I. It was also the 15th anniversary of the Beer Hall Putsch, the Nazis' unsuccessful attempt to overthrow the German government in 1923.

News of the assassination attempt was first reported on November 8, just as members of the Nazi Party were gathering in Munich, Germany, to commemorate the anniversary of the Beer Hall Putsch. Goebbels took the opportunity to fan the flames of anti-Semitism among the gathered party members by speaking about Grynszpan's attack.

In 1938, Nazis gathered in the beer hall where Hitler had attempted his 1923 putsch, to commemorate the event.

61

The Nazi propaganda ministry had instructed all of Germany's newspaper editors to make sure the story of the attack dominated the front page of every paper. Newspapers around Germany carried stories that were designed to inflame anti-Semitism in the Third Reich. Goebbels' newspaper, *Der Angriff*, ran a story that demanded, "From this vile deed arises the imperative demand for immediate action against the Jews, with most severe consequences."

Newspapers all over Germany, including Muenchner Neueste Nachrichten, *carried the story of Ernst vom Rath's assassination. A typical headline read "Jewish murder attack in the German Embassy."*

A report in the Nazi-run *Volkischer Beobachter* newspaper read:

> *It is clear that the German people will draw their own conclusion from this new deed. It is an impossible situation that within our frontiers hundreds of thousands of Jews should control our shopping streets, places of entertainment, and as "foreign" landlords pocket the money of German tenants, while their racial comrades outside call for war against Germany and shoot down German officials.*

While the Nazi papers ranted about Grynszpan's villainy and called for payback against Jews, German Jews remained publicly silent. All Jewish newspapers and magazines had been banned. The Jews of Germany had no way to comment on the event.

Hitler was told about vom Rath's death as he ate dinner in Munich's old town hall chamber. Witnesses recalled that the führer pushed his dinner away and spoke quietly to Goebbels, who was seated beside him. Goebbels later said that he and Hitler had talked about anti-Jewish riots that had taken place around Germany the night before. He said Hitler told him that although the party should not organize similar demonstrations, it should not stop any that might occur "spontaneously." Other people who were there said they heard Hitler say that "the SA should be allowed to have a fling."

Hitler then rose from the table and left the hall. This was unusual. Hitler usually gave the closing speech at these gatherings. But this was all part of Hitler and Goebbels' plan. Now no matter what was said after he left, or what happened as a result of that, Hitler could always claim that he had never given any specific orders. The job of giving the closing speech—and any orders—fell to Goebbels. He did not waste the opportunity. He said, in part:

> *I have news here for you tonight, to demonstrate what happens to a good German when he relaxes his vigil for one moment. Ernst vom Rath was a good German, a loyal servant of the Reich, working for the good of our people in our embassy in Paris. Shall I tell you what happened to him? He was shot down! In the course of his duty, he went, unarmed and unsuspecting, to speak to a visitor at the embassy, and had two bullets pumped into him. He is now dead. Do I need to tell you the race of the dirty swine who perpetrated this foul deed? A Jew! Tonight he lies in jail in Paris, claiming that he acted on his own, that he had no instigators of this awful deed behind him. But we know better, don't we? Comrades, we cannot allow this attack by international Jewry to go unchallenged. ... I ask you to listen to me, and together we must plan what is to be our answer to Jewish murder and the threat of international Jewry to our glorious German Reich!*

After hearing Goebbels' speech, the leaders of Nazi groups spread the word to their local party

members: It was not only Herschel Grynszpan who was to blame for vom Rath's death; it was all Jews—and they all needed to be punished.

Joseph Goebbels was in charge of stirring up violence against the Jews following the attack on Ernst vom Rath.

A message went out from Gestapo headquarters to all local police bureaus, alerting them that demonstrations against Jews would take place that night. The demonstrations would be orchestrated and carried out by the SA. The police were told not to interfere, except to prevent looting. They were also told to expect the arrests of 20,000 to 30,000 Jews, particularly those who were rich.

Further orders instructed police that there was to be no arson against Jewish businesses. Synagogues and community centers were to be destroyed, but businesses and homes were to remain intact. The Nazis wanted the Jews out, but they wanted their real estate and businesses protected so they could be passed on to Aryan owners. ◤

The November Pogrom

By midnight on November 9, 1938, attacks on Jewish businesses, homes, and synagogues were occurring all across the Third Reich. Mobs roamed through the streets shouting, "Beat the Jews to death."

In Munich, the first synagogue started to burn at midnight. Firefighters were on hand as the fire began to spread to a nearby Jewish schoolhouse. They attempted to control the flames, but SA officers cut their hoses and added gasoline to the fire.

In Berlin, the pogrom was delayed until 2 A.M. on November 10 so that police would have time to prepare. They identified Jewish property that would be destroyed and set up roadblocks to keep traffic away from those areas. They also wanted firefighters standing by to make sure that fires did not spread from synagogues to nearby homes or businesses. By dawn, nine of the 12 synagogues in the city were on fire.

In Cologne, Germany, the police handed out axes and other tools of destruction to members of the SA and other troublemakers in the mob. They also supplied a list of names and addresses of Jewish property to be destroyed. The police did not want to risk any Aryan property accidentally being targeted. Seventeen Jewish shops in the city center were destroyed.

Before it was destroyed during Kristallnacht, the Herzog Rudolfstrasse was a major synagogue in Munich.

In Nuremberg, the SA destroyed nearly every Jewish thing in sight before turning on the Jews themselves. In one bloody day, nine Jews were murdered. Some were beaten to death, one was thrown from the window of his house, and another was thrown down his own staircase repeatedly until he died. There were 10 suicides reported, five by women.

Anything the Nazis did not destroy, they stole. Many Jews were forced to sign over their property for a fraction of what it was worth. One example of this is a synagogue that was worth more than 100,000 reichsmarks ($24,000). It was sold for 100 reichsmarks ($24). Jewish people were told that if they did not agree to sell at these ridiculous prices, they would be killed. By November 14, most of the Jewish property in Nuremberg had been turned over to the local Nazi Party.

After Kristallnacht, life went on as usual for non-Jewish German citizens. Whether or not they approved of the destruction, few people spoke out against it.

Because the SA in Austria and the Sudetenland were eager to show their loyalty to Germany, they were particularly brutal in their attacks. Freddie Knoller, who was a schoolboy in Vienna, Austria, at the time of Kristallnacht, later recalled the terror that gripped him and his family that night:

JEWISH ATONEMENT FINE

At first, Hermann Goering did not approve of Kristallnacht because German insurance companies would have to pay for the damage to Jewish property. Together with Hitler and Goebbels, Goering decided to make the Jews themselves pay for the damage to their property. They imposed a fee of 1 billion reichsmarks ($400 million), which was called the Jewish Atonement Fine.

Somewhere around 11 that night, we heard a noise in our courtyard, and looking down we saw the Storm Troopers [SA] talking to our caretaker. He took them into the building. My mother became quite hysterical: "What are they going to do? Where are they going? Are they coming up to us?" My father turned off the lights so that the apartment was in darkness. Suddenly we heard a woman's shrill voice, a screaming voice, and we heard the glass of a window breaking. We heard a thud in the courtyard. We looked down and saw a body lying there. We didn't know who it was until the woman, Mrs. Epstein from the first floor, came running into the courtyard, screaming and going to her husband's body.

As the looting and destruction wound down on November 10, the arrests began. Jewish men of all ages were rounded up and marched through the streets as their German neighbors shouted insults at them.

During the week following Kristallnacht, 30,000 Jewish men were arrested and sent to concentration camps: 9,845 were sent to Buchenwald, 10,911 were sent to Dachau, and between 9,000 and 10,000 were sent to Sachsenhausen. Until Kristallnacht, Jewish people weren't sent to these camps simply because they were Jews.

The prisoners in the concentration camps were a forced labor crew that supplied the materials for Hitler's many building projects. Inside the camps, the prisoners were treated like animals. They were forced to stand in line in the hot sun, sometimes for 15 hours at a time. During this time, the prisoners were not given any food or water, and they were not allowed to go to the bathroom or sit down. Sometimes the guards would enter the barracks and pick prisoners at random. They would bring the prisoners outside and beat them with steel rods or clubs. Many prisoners died in this way, or from a guard's bullet. Others killed themselves by charging the electric fences.

CONCENTRATION CAMPS

Early concentration camps were designed as detention and work camps for political prisoners, other alleged "enemies" of the Nazi regime, and people who broke Reich laws. Although individual prisoners were often murdered, these camps were not death camps that housed gas chambers and crematoria. The Nazis' six death camps, Auschwitz-Birkenau, Belzec, Chelmno, Majdanek, Sobibor, and Treblinka, were built later.

The Jews who were arrested after Kristallnacht were not expected to stay long in the camps. Their imprisonment was intended to encourage them to leave Germany. The prisoners were told that they would be released as long as they were ready to leave the country immediately. Gestapo officials warned the prisoners that if they told anyone about what went on at the camps, they would immediately be arrested and returned to the camps. The officials said that prisoners were not allowed to talk about their experiences in the camps even after they left Germany. They warned the prisoners that German spies would be watching and would punish them if they spoke out against the Nazi government.

As a result of the Kristallnacht pogrom on the night of November 9 and the following day, at least 7,500 stores, 29 warehouses, and 171 houses were destroyed. They were all Jewish owned. In addition, approximately 200 synagogues were burned to the

In 1938, prisoners at camps such as the one at Sachsenhausen, Germany, worked to supply materials for Hitler's many building projects. They were often worked to death.

ground, and 76 were demolished. In all, as many as 2,500 Jews—including men, women, and children of all ages—died as a result of Kristallnacht, mostly in concentration camps.

Only a small portion of Germans actively participated in Kristallnacht. The majority were either afraid to get involved or were indifferent to the plight of the Jews. Dorothea Illigens, a non-Jew who lived in Beckum, Germany, at the time, recalled:

Nearly 300 synagogues were destroyed as a result of Kristallnacht.

> *I remember the Reichskristallnacht [the Kristallnacht pogram] well. My little son was ill with a serious eye infection and I was up and down half the night caring for him.*

Kristallnacht, November 9-10, 1938

North Sea · SWEDEN · Baltic Sea · LATVIA · LITHUANIA · DENMARK · DANZIG · Königsberg · Danzig · EAST PRUSSIA (GER.) · Kiel · Lübeck · NETHERLANDS · Hamburg · Stettin · Bremen · GERMANY · Hannover · Berlin · Beckum · Düsseldorf · Cologne · Leipzig · Dresden · Breslau · POLAND · BELGIUM · Bonn · Frankfurt · Sudetenland · LUXEMBOURG · Nuremburg · CZECHOSLOVAKIA · FRANCE · Freiburg · Munich · Linz · Vienna · Salzburg · HUNGARY · ROMAN · LIECHTENSTEIN · AUSTRIA · SWITZERLAND · YUGOSLAVIA · ITALY

0 · 75 · 150 mi.
0 · 75 · 150 km

- Cities where synagogues were des
- Former borders, 1933
- Land added to Germany, 1938

Then I heard, over and over again, in the street, walking, running, shouting, windows being broken. The SS [Nazi guards] had broken into the Jewish houses. They had driven the Jews out onto the street. They had beaten them up so badly they needed to go into [the] hospital, but no one dared to do anything about it, or to go outside. One did not quite know what was going on, but one sensed that it was something dreadful. And in the morning, no one spoke about it. Most people stayed in their homes. They were just glad not to have been involved.

Some non-Jewish Germans, such as Pastor Julius von Jan, chose to speak out. Von Jan led a Lutheran congregation in Swabia, a region of Germany. After Kristallnacht, he preached to his congregation about the evils of the pogrom:

Houses of worship, sacred to others, have been burned down with impunity [without fear of punishment]—men who have loyally served our nation and conscientiously done their duty have been thrown into concentration camps simply because they belong to a different race. Our nation's infamy is bound to bring about divine punishment.

Von Jan quickly received punishment himself for speaking out. A Nazi mob beat him and threw him onto the roof of a shed. As had happened to so many Jews on November 9, the pastor's house was then destroyed, and he was thrown in jail. ◼

The Aftermath

Chapter

8

The rest of the world saw what happened in Germany on November 9 and 10, and people were outraged. Newspapers from almost every country ran anti-Nazi stories and showed sympathy for the Jewish victims.

During a press conference called by Goebbels for foreign correspondents in Berlin on November 11, the propaganda minister said that the Kristallnacht demonstrations had been the unplanned reactions of the German people to vom Rath's assassination. However, none of the reporters present were satisfied with Goebbels' words, and they continued to press him for the truth.

For once, Goebbels was shaken. He insisted that if Jews around the world continued to spread exaggerations about the event—as he

claimed they had been doing in American news stories—"they would be digging the graves of Jews in Germany."

As usual, the Nazis planned to use fear as their weapon. They thought that threats against the Jews who were still living in Germany would silence foreign critics of the Nazi government. The Nazis also hoped that being forthright about their plans to get rid of the Jews would encourage other nations to find a place for Jewish refugees.

The Tielshafer Synagogue in Berlin was burned during Kristallnacht and later bombed during World War II.

A British official reported back to his government that, right after the pogrom, a high-ranking Nazi official told him:

> *Germany intended to get rid of her Jews, either by emigration or if necessary by starving or killing them, since she would not risk having such a hostile minority in the country in the event of war.*

He also said, "Germany intended to expel or kill all of the Jews in Poland, Hungary, and the Ukraine when she took control of those countries."

But despite the world's outrage over Kristallnacht and the clear message about the Nazis' plans for the Jews, no other country came forward to intervene. British Prime Minister Neville Chamberlain still refused to speak out against Hitler, even though members of the press and the British Parliament pressed him to do so. The subject was never even raised in the French government.

KINDERTRANSPORT

After Kristallnacht, the British Jewish Refugee Committee appealed to members of Parliament to allow German immigrants into the country. After much debate, it was decided that an unspecified number of children ages 17 and younger would be allowed into Great Britain. This program was known as Kindertransport. The first transport left Germany less than one month after Kristallnacht. About 10,000 children made the trip between that time and when the program ended on September 3, 1939. When the children arrived in Great Britain, some were sent to orphanages or group homes, some were taken in by foster families, and others worked on farms. Most of the children never saw their families again.

Even the response from other Jews around the world was muted. Three days after Kristallnacht, representatives of the General Jewish Council met in New York to discuss a response to the pogrom. According to a report in *The Jewish Week*, the members of the council were worried about anti-Semitism in the United States and decided "that there should be no parades, public demonstrations or protests by Jews."

Only one day after the press conference he called, Goebbels was back to business as usual. He felt that the Nazis had gotten away with Kristallnacht and was confident that no matter what they did to the Jews, there would be no consequences.

The Nazis tried to humiliate Jews any way they could—for example, by shaving the beard of an Orthodox Jew. Orthodox Jews believe it is against Jewish law to shave.

On November 14, the Nazis published new decrees. Jews had been excluded from cultural events before, but they were now prohibited by law from attending concerts, movies, and other performances. "It is equivalent to degradation of German art to expect a German to sit next to a Jew in a theater or cinema," said Goebbels. On November 15, German Education Minister Bernhard Rust issued an order that banned all Jewish children from German schools. "After the ruthless murder in Paris, no German teacher can any longer be asked to give lessons to Jewish schoolchildren," he said in a press interview. "It goes without saying that it is intolerable for German pupils to sit in the same classroom with Jews."

That same day, U.S. President Franklin D. Roosevelt became the first and only world leader to publicly speak out against the Nazi government. In a speech given on November 15, he said:

> *The news of the last few days from Germany has deeply shocked public opinion in the United States. Such news from any part of the world would inevitably produce a similar profound reaction among American people in every part of the nation. I myself could scarcely believe that such things could occur in a twentieth-century civilization.*

Roosevelt then recalled the American ambassador from Berlin—something that had not happened since World War I. But the situation for Jews in Germany continued to worsen.

On November 28, detailed regulations were announced for the Aryanization of all Jewish businesses. That same day, regulations restricting the movement of Jews in public places were also announced. Starting on December 6, Jews were forbidden to walk or drive in certain places. In Berlin, the ban covered all public recreational facilities, including theaters, concert halls, museums, parks, and swimming pools. Any Jew who was caught in one of these banned places could be fined 150 reichsmarks ($36) or spend six weeks in prison.

Jews were also forbidden to walk on many of the streets in Berlin. Jewish people who lived on the banned streets were told to pack their bags and look for somewhere else to live. Hotel owners asked for a decree that would ban Jews from their establishments. Soon other cities and towns enacted similar restrictions. The first steps were being taken toward the creation of Jewish ghettos. Once again, the new laws were enacted before the eyes of the world. The Nazis were clear about their intentions. They wanted the Jews to leave Germany.

GHETTOS

After the start of World War II, the Nazis concentrated Jewish populations in designated areas of a city called ghettos. Jewish people lived in miserable conditions in ghettos, isolated from the non-Jewish community. The Germans and their allies created more than 800 ghettos in Eastern Europe. At least 1 million Jews were forced to live in them.

The Nazis continued to use threats of further violence against German Jews to ensure that no one would interfere with their plans. Perhaps that is what kept the rest of the world from acting. But there can be no denying that many countries were unwilling to upset international trade, risk involvement in another war, or create policy problems at home.

Hitler nullified Germany's nonaggression pact with Poland during an April 1939 session of the Reichstag.

It's impossible to say whether anything—except another world war—could have made Hitler stray from his path. But perhaps if the rest the world had acted, the disaster that was just on the horizon could have been avoided.

Eventually, war did come to Europe. On September 1, 1939, Germany invaded Poland. Great Britain and France declared war on Germany on September 3. World War II had begun.

Germany had become an awesome military power that the rest of the world was not prepared to fight. By June 1941, the Nazi empire covered most of Europe as the German army marched across the continent, meeting little real resistance. By the time the United States entered the fray at the end of that year, Great Britain and the Soviet Union were the only nations still able to put up a fight. Together, Great Britain, the Soviet Union, and the United States (the Allied powers) led the fight against Germany, Japan, and Italy (the Axis powers).

At the same time the Germans were expanding their empire, they were increasing the number of "undesirables" within that empire. Forcing Jews to emigrate or placing them in concentration camps was no longer enough for them. The regime considered a plan to transport the Jews of Europe to the island of Madagascar, off the coast of Africa, but the course of the war made this impossible. The Nazis needed a new plan—what they called "the Final Solution" to the Jewish question. That solution was genocide—an attempt to wipe out the entire Jewish population. This policy of genocide would come to be known as the Holocaust.

When the Nazis took over Poland, they suddenly had millions of Jews in their control. The first wave of killings was carried out by special execution squads that followed the regular German army into Poland—as well as local populations willing to cooperate with the Germans. The main targets were male Jews, communists, and members of the Polish economic and cultural elite.

The execution squads would round up the people they wanted to kill, bring them to the outskirts of town, and force them to dig mass graves. Then they would line their victims up on the edge of the graves and mow them down with machine guns. Before the end of the war, women and children would be among the victims of these execution squads.

As the Germans advanced on the Soviet Union, millions more Jews came under their control. A new method was devised for killing these people. They were placed in vans that were built so that the vehicles' exhaust would blow into the vans. The people inside were gassed to death within 15 minutes.

Before long, the Nazis realized that these methods of killing Jews were inefficient. In the late summer of 1941, Hitler made the decision that all the Jews of Europe were to be killed. This policy was coordinated at the highest levels of the Nazi Party and government at a conference in Wannsee, a suburb of Berlin. In January 1942, the Nazis came up with the plan to expand some of their concentration camps into extermination camps.

The Germans and their allies in Europe rounded up Jews anywhere they could find them and sent them to extermination camps, which were equipped with gas chambers. The prisoners were also shot, beaten to death, and hanged. Of the 6 million Jews who were murdered by the Nazis, more than half met their end in one of these camps.

When Allied forces liberated camps, such as the one at Dachau, they began to understand the true horrors of the Holocaust.

In July 1944, Majdanek in Poland was the first death camp liberated by Soviet troops. Andrew Werth, a correspondent for *The Times* of London and the British Broadcasting Corporation (BBC), took a tour of Majdanek one month after the liberation. His bosses at the BBC refused to air his report, though. It was so hard to imagine the horrors that had occurred in these camps that they

A Kristallnacht memorial was erected in Berlin after World War II.

thought Werth's story was based on propaganda made up by the Soviets. It was not until more camps were liberated that people began to understand and believe what had been happening.

Although most people did not know what was going on inside these camps, Allied leaders did. The only solution they could find to ending the genocide, though, was to defeat Germany as quickly as possible. They believed that winning the war was the only way to end the Holocaust.

The Allies ultimately did win the war, but Hitler was never made to pay for his crimes. He shot himself on April 30, 1945, as the Soviet army was advancing on his bunker in Berlin. The next day, Goebbels killed himself and ordered the death of his children.

In 1945, after the war ended, a special court was created to try top Nazi officials for their crimes during the war. The International Military Tribunal at Nuremberg was convened in November of that year. It was during these trials that much of the evidence about the planning of Kristallnacht became public. Eleven of the defendants at Nuremberg were condemned to death, including Goering. However, Goering killed himself on October 14, 1946, the day before he was scheduled to be hanged. ◣

WHAT BECAME OF HERSCHEL GRYNSZPAN

Herschel Grynszpan was never tried for his crime. The French government was afraid to act—if a jury found Grynszpan not guilty, France would feel the wrath of the Nazis. When Germany invaded France, Grynszpan was transferred to Sachsenhausen. The Nazis intended to use Grynszpan's trial as a propaganda tool, so he was well cared for in prison. They were never able to make the trial happen on their terms, though. Grynszpan spent most of the war at Sachsenhausen, and by 1942 his name disappeared from the German record books. No one knows for sure what happened to him, but most people suspect he died in the camp.

Timeline

November 11, 1918

World War I officially ends.

November 8–9, 1923

A group of armed Nazi Party members led by Adolf Hitler try to overtake the German government but fail.

May 10, 1933

Books by Jewish authors and others the Nazis disapprove of are burned throughout Germany.

September 15, 1935

Nuremberg Laws are enacted.

March 13, 1938

Anschluss, or annexation, of Austria occurs.

April 22, 1938

Decree is passed requiring declaration of all Jewish property valued at more than 5,000 reichsmarks.

June 9, 1938

Main synagogue in Munich, Germany, is burned down.

June 14, 1938

Decree is issued requiring the identification and registration of all Jewish industrial businesses.

July 15, 1938

International conference to discuss the issue of Jewish refugees takes place in Evian, France.

July 21, 1938

Identity cards for Jews are intoduced.

July 28, 1938

Decree is introduced announcing the cancellation of medical certification for all Jewish doctors.

August 10, 1938

Synagogue in Nuremberg, Germany, is burned down.

August 17, 1938

Decree is issued requiring Jews to add the names Israel and Sarah to their first names.

September 12, 1938

Jews are forbidden to attend cultural events.

September 27, 1938

Jewish attorneys are forbidden from practicing law.

October 7, 1938

Jewish passports are revoked, and identity cards are issued.

October 28, 1938

12,000 Jews of Polish origin are expelled to Zbonszyn.

November 7, 1938

Herschel Grynszpan shoots Ernst vom Rath.

November 9, 1938

Ernst vom Rath dies; Joseph Goebbels gives the closing speech during events commemorating the Beer Hall Putsch and blames all Jews for vom Rath's death.

November 9–10, 1938

Jewish businesses, homes, and synagogues are attacked during Kristallnacht.

Midnight

Synagogues and stores in Munich are burned.

1 A.M.

Killing and looting occur in Leslum, Germany.

2 A.M.

The pogrom begins in Berlin; first Munich death is reported to Goebbels.

2:50 A.M.

On Hitler's orders, the police in Munich order a stop to the pogrom.

4 A.M.

Synagogues in Cologne, Germany, are set on fire.

5 A.M.

SA sets fire to principal synagogues in Frankfurt-am-Main.

6 A.M.

Jewish shops and houses in Cologne are destroyed.

6:30 A.M.

Nazi storm troopers begin to destroy Jewish homes in Frankfurt-am-Main, Germany.

8 A.M.

Mobs ordered to move out from Cologne into the suburbs of Lindenthal and Sülz.

1 P.M.

All destructive activity in Cologne is scheduled to end.

November 11, 1938

Goebbels holds a press conference for foreign correspondents.

November 12, 1938

Decree is issued demanding "atonement payments" from German Jews for Kristallnacht damages.

Timeline

November 14, 1938

Jewish children are banned from
German public schools.

November 28, 1938

Regulations are announced for the
Aryanization of Jewish businesses.

December 6, 1938

 Jews are
forbidden to
drive or walk in
certain places.

September 1–3, 1939

Germany invades Poland, and World
War II begins.

Summer 1941

Hitler decides that all Jews of Europe
are to be killed.

July 1944

The first death camp is liberated.

ON THE WEB

For more information on this topic, use FactHound.

1 Go to *www.facthound.com*

2 Type in this book ID: 0756534895

3 Click on the *Fetch It!* button. FactHound will find the best Web sites for you.

HISTORIC SITES

United States Holocaust Memorial Museum
100 Raoul Wallenberg Place
Washington, DC 20024
202/488-0400

Learn about life in Nazi Germany and the Holocaust through first-person accounts and stunning exhibits.

Zekelman Family Holocaust Memorial Center
28123 Orchard Lake Road
Farmington Hills, MI 48334-3788
248/553-2400

Visitors can see the Kristallnacht Mosaic on display.

LOOK FOR MORE BOOKS IN THIS SERIES

Black Tuesday:
Prelude to the Great Depression

The Berlin Airlift:
Breaking the Soviet Blockade

The Cultural Revolution:
Years of Chaos in China

A Day Without Immigrants:
Rallying Behind America's Newcomers

The Iran-Contra Affair:
Political Scandal Uncovered

The March on Washington:
Uniting Against Racism

A complete list of **Snapshots in History** titles is available on our Web site: *www.compasspointbooks.com*

Glossary

Allies
friends or helpers; when capitalized, refers to the United States and its allies during major wars

anti-Semitic
discrimination against or persecution of Jewish people

Aryan
term used by Nazis to describe a supposed master race of pure-blooded Germans with blond hair and blue eyes

assassination
murder of someone who is well known or important, often for political reasons

atonement
compensation for a wrongdoing

chancellor
the head of government in some countries, such as Germany

democratic
government system run by officials elected by citizens

dictator
ruler who takes complete control of a country, often unjustly

discrimination
treating someone badly because he or she is different

emigrate
to leave a home country to settle in another country permanently

Evian Conference
conference held to help political refugees emigrate from Austria and Germany, but which achieved little

fascism
form of government that promotes extreme nationalism, repression, and anticommunism, and is ruled by a dictator

führer
German word meaning "leader"

Gestapo
German secret police

Jew
person whose religion is Judaism

Nazi
a member of the National Socialist Party led by Adolf Hitler

Orthodox Jew
person who strictly follows Jewish law

pogrom
an organized attack on a minority group, especially Jews

racist
one who hates other people based solely on their race

swastika
an ancient religious symbol that became the Nazi emblem

Third Reich
official name of Hitler's regime, which ruled Germany from 1933 to 1945

Treaty of Versailles
agreement signed by the Allies and Germans in Versailles, France, that ended World War I

Source Notes

Chapter 1
Page 10, line 25: *The Nazis: A Warning from History.* Laurence Rees and Tilman Remme. British Broadcasting Corporation, 1997.

Page 12, line 5: Anthony Read and David Fisher. *Kristallnacht: The Nazi Night of Terror.* New York: Random House, 1989, p. 68.

Chapter 3
Page 31, line 9: Marion A. Kaplan. *Between Dignity and Despair: Jewish Life in Nazi Germany.* New York: Oxford University Press, 1998, pp. 33–34.

Page 35, line 10: Ibid., p. 35.

Chapter 4
Page 44, line 3: *Kristallnacht: The Nazi Night of Terror,* p. 28.

Page 51, line 9: Ibid., p. 30.

Page 53, line 2: Ibid.

Chapter 5
Page 54, line 14: ZStA Potsdam, Reichspropagandaministerium File 991, 61–64; CDJ 13:8312.

Page 56, line 11: *Kristallnacht: The Nazi Night of Terror,* p. 40.

Page 57, sidebar: *Kristallnacht: The Nazi Night of Terror,* p. 51.

Page 57, line 30: Gerald Schwab. *The Day the Holocaust Began: The Odyssey of Herschel Grynszpan.* New York: Praeger, 1990, p. 4.

Page 59, line 7: *Kristallnacht: The Nazi Night of Terror,* p. 7.

Chapter 6
Page 62, line 7: Ibid., p. 61.

Page 63, line 3 and 30: Ibid., pp. 61 and 62.

Page 64, line 10: "The Trial of German Major War Criminals Sitting at Nuremberg, Germany 16th April to 1st May, 1946 One-Hundred-and-Sixteenth Day: Monday, 29th April, 1946," p. 349.

Chapter 7
Page 69, line 12: Lyn Smith. *Remembering: Voices of the Holocaust.* New York: Carroll & Graf Publishers, 2005, p. 50.

Page 72, line 10: *Kristallnacht: The Nazi Night of Terror,* p. 123.

Page 73, line 19: Ibid., p. 125.

SOURCE NOTES

Chapter 8

Page 75, line 2: British Foreign Office papers, Public Record Office 371/21637.

Page 76, line 4: British Foreign Office papers, Public Record Office 371/21638.

Page 77, line 8: Rafael Medoff. "Kristallnacht—and the World's Response." The David S. Wyman Institute for Holocaust Studies, November 2003.

Page 78, line 5: *Kristallnacht: The Nazi Night of Terror,* p. 165.

Page 78, line 10: Ibid., p. 165.

Page 78, line 20: Ibid., p. 171.

SELECT BIBLIOGRAPHY

Kaplan, Marion A. *Between Dignity and Despair: Jewish Life in Nazi Germany.* New York: Oxford University Press, 1998.

Laqueur, Walter. *Generation Exodus: The Fate of Young Jewish Refugees from Nazi Germany.* Hanover, N.H.: Brandeis University Press, 2001.

Read, Anthony, and David Fisher *Kristallnacht: The Nazi Night of Terror.* New York: Random House, 1989.

Schwab, Gerald. *The Day the Holocaust Began: The Odyssey of Herschel Grynszpan.* New York: Praeger, 1990.

Smith, Lyn. *Remembering: Voices of the Holocaust.* New York: Carroll & Graf Publishers, 2005.

FURTHER READING

Altman, Linda Jacobs. *The Holocaust, Hitler, and Nazi Germany.* Springfield, N.J.: Enslow Publishers, 1999.

Gottfried, Ted. *Nazi Germany.* Brookfield, Conn.: Millbrook Press, 2000.

Haugen, Brenda. *Adolf Hitler: Dictator of Nazi Germany.* Minneapolis: Compass Point Books, 2006.

Kertzer, Morris N. *What is a Jew?* Rev. by Lawrence A. Hoffman. New York: Maxwell Macmillan International, 1993.

Matas, Carol. *Daniel's Story.* New York: Scholastic, 1993.

Perl, Lila, and Marion Blumenthal Lazan. *Four Perfect Pebbles: A Holocaust Story.* New York: Greenwillow Books, 1996.

Index

About the Author

Stephanie Fitzgerald has been writing nonfiction for children for more than 10 years. Her specialties include history, wildlife, and popular culture. Stephanie is currently working on a picture book with the help of her daughter, Molly.

Image Credits

Mary Evans/Weimar Archive **cover**, akg-images pp. 21 (Bettman), 41, 5 and 58; Corbis pp. 9, 29, 39, 61 (Hulton-Deutsch Collection), 23, 48–49, 68, 71 (Bettmann), 85 (Ira Nowinski), 52; Getty Images pp.14, 25 (Hulton Archive), 17 (General Photographic Agency), 19 (Henry Guttman), 6 and 31, 34 and 86, 43, 44 (Keystone), **back cover (middle)** 36 (Anthony Potter Collection), 50 (Pictorial Parade), 65 (Keystone), 77 and 88 (Imagno/Austrian Archives), 83 (Time & Life Pictures), **back cover (right)** and 75, 80; The United States Holocaust Memorial Museum **back cover (left)** and 12, pp. 2 (courtesy of National Archives and Records Administration, College Park), 26 and 86 (courtesy of Joseph Shadur), 55 and 87 (courtesy of Hanna Rawicz Keselman), 62 (courtesy of Muenchner Neueste Nachrichten), 67 and 86 (courtesy of Steven Frank), 11; Weimar Archive cover (Mary Evans).